The hottest sta

Cyndi Lauper
Culture Club
Wham!
Eurythmics
Billy Joel
Lionel Richie
Quiet Riot
The Cars
Hall and Oates
Prince
Billy Idol
The Police
Pat Benatar
Van Halen
Madonna
Duran Duran
Michael Jackson
"Weird Al" Yankovic
David Bowie
Frankie Goes to Hollywood
Twisted Sister
Bruce Springsteen

. . . and many more! This up-to-date guide tells you all about the stars who make television rock. This is *the* source of information on all the biggest stars and all their greatest videos!

Most Archway Paperbacks are available at special quantity discounts for bulk purchases for sales promotions, premiums or fund raising. Special books or book excerpts can also be created to fit specific needs.

For details write the office of the Vice President of Special Markets, Pocket Books, 1230 Avenue of the Americas, New York, New York 10020.

ROCK
VIDEO
SUPERSTARS

DANIEL AND SUSAN COHEN

AN ARCHWAY PAPERBACK
Published by POCKET BOOKS • NEW YORK

The authors would like to thank the following people for all their help: Cecily Harrison, MTV; Vicky Rose, The Howard Bloom Organization; Debra Kresh, The Press Office, Ltd.; Harriet Sternberg, Kragen and Company; Mary Jo Mysezelow, RCA, Joanne Browne and Kathryn Schenker, A&M Records; Steve Mandel, Van Halen Productions; Gail Davis and Jennifer Light, Isolar; Jay Levey, Imaginary Entertainment; Marilyn Laverty, CBS Records; Melinda Cooper, Freddy DeMann; Warren Entner; Linda Karp, Rogers and Cowan, Inc.; Elliot Roberts, Lookout Management; Dana Morris, Newstar Enterprise.

AN ARCHWAY PAPERBACK *Original*

An Archway Paperback published by
POCKET BOOKS, a division of Simon & Schuster, Inc.
1230 Avenue of the Americas, New York, N.Y. 10020

Copyright © 1985 by Daniel and Susan Cohen
Cover photograph of Cyndi Lauper © 1985 Debra A. Trebitz/
Lynn Goldsmith, Inc.
Cover photograph of Prince © 1985 Roger Jones
Cover photograph of Madonna by Ron Wolfson/
Lynn Goldsmith, Inc.
Cover photograph of David Lee Roth by Raj Rama/
Lynn Goldsmith, Inc.

All rights reserved, including the right to reproduce
this book or portions thereof in any form whatsoever.
For information address Pocket Books, 1230 Avenue
of the Americas, New York, N.Y. 10020

ISBN: 0-671-55831-5

First Archway Paperback printing July, 1985

10 9 8 7 6 5 4 3 2

AN ARCHWAY PAPERBACK and colophon are
registered trademarks of Simon & Schuster, Inc.

Printed in the U.S.A.

IL 4+

CONTENTS

ESTABLISHED STARS

FUTURE STARS

THE ROCK VIDEO REVOLUTION

It's hard to imagine the world today without rock video. It's everywhere. Besides MTV—the twenty-four-hour-a-day rock video cable channel—there are hundreds of other local and national programs that feature the spectacular combinations of sound and sight. There are rock video clubs and video jukeboxes. Videos have influenced films, advertising, and fashion. They have pumped new life into a sagging record industry.

Most of all, the videos have given us a host of new superstars. Cyndi Lauper, Duran Duran, Madonna, and many others owe their fame to videos. Michael Jackson had been a star before videos, but it was the videos that made him the most popular entertainer in the world.

It's been a revolution. But when did it begin? And why?

1

In a sense, the rock video revolution began on August 1, 1981. That's when MTV first began its round-the-clock operations. It was a gamble. MTV reached only four million homes, just a handful in TV terms. It didn't even get into New York City. MTV execs had to go over the George Washington Bridge to Fort Lee, New Jersey, to see their new baby.

The first video shown on MTV came from England. It was by a group called the Buggles and was directed by video pioneer Russell Mulcahy. The song was called "Video Killed the Radio Star." The song had lyrics like this: "We can't rewind, we've gone too far/Put the blame on VTR." That stands for video tape recorder. (In America we call it the VCR, video cassette recorder.) One of the shots in the video shows TV sets crashing through a pile of old radios.

That's what the people who had put their money and reputations in back of MTV hoped would happen. But in the late summer of 1981 the success of MTV was far from a sure thing. There had been lots of new cable channels, and most of them had flopped.

MTV did a lot of promotion. Ads with big stars like Mick Jagger and Pat Benatar shouting "I want my MTV!" began appearing on regular TV. Soon lots of people were demanding MTV. It quickly grew into the most successful cable-TV channel of all. It's a huge money-maker.

Two people who are very happy about videos, "Weird Al" Yankovic and Cyndi Lauper.

John Bellissimo

But MTV is just a place videos can be shown. Where did the videos themselves come from? You might start way back in 1927. That's when the first "talkie," *The Jazz Singer,* came out. It was really a silent picture with a couple of Al Jolson musical numbers thrown in. But it changed the movies forever. It also shows you that pictures and music go back a long way together.

TV and rock music hit the public at about the same time. Rock greats like Elvis Presley and the Beatles made spectacular TV appearances. In general, though, there wasn't much rock on TV.

The Beatles were pioneers in videos. By 1967 they were big enough to stop touring. But fans still wanted to see them. So they made short films to promote a couple of their new songs, "Strawberry Fields Forever" and "Penny. Lane." The next year they did a short tape for "Hey Jude." The films were shipped out to TV stations all over the world.

The Beatles were always special. For a long time other rock stars didn't make short films or videos to promote their records. At least they didn't in America. In Britain, and in parts of Europe and Australia, it was different. In many countries, programs that regularly show videos have been around for a long time. Rock stars in those countries have been making videos for over ten years. That's probably why British and Aus-

4

Devo, Video Pioneers
Courtesy Lookout Management

tralian groups are so big in American videos today. They've simply had more experience.

There were a few U.S. groups like Devo that
got into videos early. But their stuff looked
strange, and nobody would show it. Comedian
Dan Ackroyd, who was then on the TV show
Saturday Night Live, was sent a Devo video in
1975. He threw it in the wastebasket.

As long as there were only a few broadcast
channels available, rock video didn't have a
chance. Then along came cable. With cable there
were loads of channels available. There were
cable channels devoted to news and sports. Why
not one to video music? That's how MTV was
born. Not even the founders who hopefully
played "Video Killed the Radio Star" knew how
big and powerful their baby would become.

The group Silent Treatment shooting a video.
Courtesy The Press Office, Ltd.

People wanted to see their favorite rock stars as well as hear them. And if they liked what they saw and heard, they went out and bought the records. That made everyone sit up and take notice.

Before MTV, the way to sell records was to get the songs played on the radio and then to go out on tour. But groups like Duran Duran—who had little if any radio exposure and who had never toured in the U.S.—began selling records like crazy in cities that had MTV. Cyndi Lauper had been singing her heart out in dives. She never had a hit record. She never even had a record. Then came the video for "Girls Just Wanna Have Fun." Her first album went platinum and her concerts sold out everywhere. Madonna has rarely even given a concert. Yet in 1985 she was the fastest-rising star around. It's all due to videos.

A cameraman quoted in *The Rolling Stone*

Book of Rock Video recalls: "In the days before MTV, making videos was seen by the bands as a hassle. They'd show up and do a few takes, but after that they couldn't be bothered. If anyone complained they'd say, 'Hey, man, we're rock stars, not film stars.'" That doesn't happen very much anymore.

Just making a video and appearing on MTV doesn't guarantee success. And there are groups that sell records and pack concert halls without the aid of videos. But everyone connected with rock will tell you that videos have just stood the whole music business on its head.

It's a bit like what happened after Al Jolson stepped out there in *The Jazz Singer* in 1927. Some big stars of silent films just couldn't make it in talkies. Others made the change with ease. And since the talkies brought more people than ever into the films, there was room for a whole new and even bigger crop of stars. That's what's happening in rock right now.

"There probably isn't a record in the top fifty that hasn't got a video," says veteran rock star Mick Jagger of the Rolling Stones. Simon Le Bon of Duran Duran, a group that owes much of its success to videos, says, "I take video seriously. I see it as an art form. Videos are the talking pictures of today's music industry."

We're going to take a look at those who are really making it in the world of rock video.

CYNDI LAUPER

Call her Cyndi for Cinderella. Only a couple of years ago she was an unknown. Cyndi barely earned enough money singing in New York City clubs to pay her rent. Oh sure, she had a small number of fans. After all, Cyndi had always been unusual, and somebody was bound to notice the funny, bubbly five-foot-three-inch singer with the flaming pink-orange-red hair who wore tons of jewelry and brightly colored clothes.

Then there was Cyndi's voice. Many rock singers have a small range. That means they have trouble hitting very high or very low notes. Not Cyndi. Besides owning a voice that soars and dips easily, Cyndi knows how to make a song sound the way it should—sad, mad, or giggly. Cyndi writes songs, too. And she has the energy, drive, and liveliness that go with being a star. Even her speaking voice is special. When Cyndi talks she reminds a lot of people of cartoon characters like Popeye's girlfriend Olive Oyl, Tweety Bird, or even Donald Duck. Others say she sounds like a little girl, but a little girl with a big New York accent.

Still, with all Cyndi had going for her to make her a star, she wasn't one. Even two months after Portrait Records released her first solo album, *She's So Unusual,* Cyndi opened for the Kinks at the Roseland Ballroom in New York. That was on December 29, 1983.

Yet only a few months later, in April 1984, Cyndi Lauper was a smash hit as the main performer at New York's leading rock club, the Ritz. She was a guest on television talk shows like *The Tonight Show* with Johnny Carson. She also made a lot of television appearances with three-hundred-pound wrestling manager Captain Lou Albano. Little Cyndi and huge Lou made quite a pair, and their zany humor went over big with the fans. Her record was selling like crazy. In February, 1985, she won the prestigious Grammy Award for Best New Artist. Everywhere she went people recognized her and asked for her autograph. What had made the difference for Cyndi? What had turned her into a star?

Cyndi zoomed like a rocket to the top of rock thanks to a music video called "Girls Just Wanna Have Fun." Weird, in a sweet kind of goofy way, it became a favorite on MTV. Captain Lou Albano was in it. So was Cyndi's mother. The un-

Cyndi Lauper
John Bellissimo

usual Ms. Lauper, born in Brooklyn, New York, in 1953, had made it big at last.

Life had never been easy for Cyndi. Her parents were hardworking people, but they didn't have much money. Her parents divorced when she was five, and she moved with her mother and sister and brother to Queens, another part of New York City.

10

Being unusual meant it was hard for Cyndi to fit in easily anywhere. She had her own ideas about how to dress. She wasn't happy in school and she wasn't a good student. She didn't want to be a waitress like her mother, though she was very close to her and still is. She didn't want to get married while she was a teenager like a lot of girls she knew. But what did she want? At seventeen Cyndi left home to find out.

If there was one thing Cyndi Lauper did like, it was music. If there was one thing she could do, it was sing. Beginning as a backup singer with a disco band, she moved on to her true love, rock. She performed in suburbs outside New York City. But if life in Queens had been hard, well, life in the world of rock was hard, too. It was especially hard for girls. Rock musicians, the people who play guitars, saxophones, and other instruments, are mostly men. So are the singers. Though Cyndi's looks are interesting, she's not what you'd call beautiful. She couldn't count on being pretty to win over fans. What Cyndi has is talent, but would the world ever see it?

Then, in 1977, something so terrible happened Cyndi thought her career was over. Just as you can wear out a jacket, you can wear out a voice. Cyndi had been singing too much and too loud. Her vocal chords couldn't take it. She lost the ability to sing.

Luckily, she found a voice coach to help her.

Cyndi and her mother at the MTV Awards.
Mark Weiss

After a lot of work Cyndi learned to sing again, better than ever. She made it to Manhattan, too. That's the one part of New York where singers really want to be. Soon Cyndi helped form a band called Blue Angel. The band got as far as making a record called "Blue Angel." It came out (or, as record companies say, was released) in 1980. The record was not a big hit. But Cyndi went right on singing songs. Blue Angel went right on playing music. No one in the band, however, Cyndi included, was making enough money to live on.

Sooner or later most bands grow tired. The excitement and newness fade. When that happens bands usually break up. In 1983 Blue Angel broke up. Cyndi got jobs singing in clubs whenever she could. She also sold clothes. Then she got a chance to make a solo album. To promote it she did a low-budget video paid for by the record company. It was the first one she'd ever made. Its success surprised a lot of people and made them realize how popular videos had become.

"Girls Just Wanna Have Fun" was followed by the sad and bittersweet "Time After Time." It tells the story of a girl who feels she must leave the town she grew up in because she's outgrown it. In the video, Cyndi's manager, David Wolff, played the boyfriend she said good-bye to. Once again her mother was played by her real-life mother. Cyndi hadn't forgotten the people who had stood by her and helped her when times were tough.

Today Cyndi is famous. When she goes on tour fans flock to see her in concert. Movies, television shows—Cyndi Lauper can do what she wants. Like Cinderella's, her dreams came true, thanks to videos.

To get in touch with Cyndi write:

Cyndi Lauper Fan Club
c/o Sixty-Five West Entertainment Co., Inc.
65 West 55th Street, Suite 4G
New York, NY 10019

DURAN DURAN

Ask the average teenaged girl to name the five most gorgeous rock stars in the world, and chances are she'll name Andy Taylor, Roger Taylor, John Taylor, Simon Le Bon, and Nick Rhodes. They're the photogenic "fab five," the rock group Duran Duran. Duran Duran are the top fashion setters to come out of Britain in years. The way they wear their hair, the way they dress, affects millions of people. Nobody has caught the look of the eighties better than Duran Duran, whose beautiful state-of-the-art rock videos have set the music industry abuzz.

Every Duranie (total Duran Duran fan) wishes she could meet and maybe go out with her own special double Duran. The Durans make the kind of videos girls love. Usually set in exotic places, they're romantic minimovies, escapes into daydreams. The videos are generally expensive and look it. They're very carefully made and show it.

Duran Duran

© 1983, Tritec Music Ltd., Photograph by Brian Aris

Duran Duran use the latest techniques in making videos, the most modern equipment, the very best talent. One of the most important names in video and advertising is Russell Mulcahy. He frequently directs Duran Duran videos.

It takes a band with class to make videos with class, and the Durans have taste, style, and glamor. They are the most up-to-date users of video around. They once did a tour only of video clubs. Huge screens showing videos are a basic and exciting feature of Duran Duran's live concerts. They've released superpopular album-length videos and set sales figures blazing with

Sony Video 45s. Duran Duran sells records at a dazzling rate, too. But in America it wasn't until fans got a good look at the sensational Durans via videos that their records really took off. Then and only then did the "Durandemonium" that had already swept through Britain, Australia, Japan, and Europe whirl through America. Films are a part of the group's future plans.

Duran Duran got its start in 1978 in Birmingham, England, where bassist John Taylor, age eighteen, and keyboard player sixteen-year-old Nick Rhodes were friends. The two decided to form a band. Since they were fans of the cult sci-fi film *Barbarella,* they named the band after the movie's villain, Durand Durand. They just chopped the last *d*'s off his name.

Simon Le Bon and Nick Rhodes of Duran Duran.
John Bellissimo

Duran Duran had more than their share of troubles for the next couple of years. Dozens of musicians joined the band and left. Somehow the combination just wasn't right. Then along came drummer Roger Taylor. Despite having the same last name, Roger and John are not related. Neither is the other Taylor, guitarist Andy, who was the last member to complete the band. In between the arrival of Roger and Andy, Simon Le Bon showed up. He was a drama student at the University of Birmingham who learned about Duran Duran from his girlfriend. She had told him she knew of a band looking for a singer. When he auditioned, there was no reason to look any further. The Duran Duran success story was about to begin.

Duran Duran recorded their first single, "Planet Earth," in 1981. In Britain new romanticism was just coming into fashion in rock. New romantics wore elegant ruffled clothes, looked like models, and went in big for synthesizer-based music. Who better than Duran Duran for new romanticism? What's more, the Durans quickly realized that their style would come across well in videos. A video clip for "Planet Earth" promoted the record straight onto the top-twenty hit list in England.

When the video "Hungry like the Wolf" made Duranies out of MTV viewers, John Taylor said, "Pop music has now become three-dimensional." Rock was no longer pure sound. Now appear-

Simon Le Bon of Duran Duran

John Bellissimo

ances would count as much and maybe more. So Duran Duran kept the great videos flowing. "Wild Boys," with its amazing color, dancing, and images, is an example of the band at its best. The "Wild Boys" video is a masterpiece. But then, who can help watching any Duran Duran video?

When fans aren't watching Duran Duran, they're listening to them. The band calls their music night music. It's music meant for dancing, though it's also nice just to hear. Melodic, energetic, and rhythmic, the songs Duran Duran play are a mixture of disco, rock 'n' roll, and rhythm and blues. There is no serious message to Duran Duran's music, though the words to their songs are often poetic.

What are the fab five like? Well, Simon Le Bon was born in 1958 and grew up near London. He went to the same school as another famous rock personality, Elton John. Simon is a science-fiction fan and he likes to draw. He loves movies. Andy Taylor was born in 1961 and grew up in northwest England, where his father was a fisherman. He started playing guitar at age five. Even during Duran Duran rehearsal breaks he likes to toss out crazed rock solos. He's married to the band's ex-hairdresser and lives in a fifteenth-century English cottage.

John Taylor was born Nigel John Taylor in 1960. More than any of the rest of Duran Duran he loves to party. He's also a James Bond fan and is crazy about fancy cars. He's warm and likable and the key person in putting Duran Duran together. Roger Taylor is the shy, quiet one in the group. He was born in 1960 in a working-class part of Birmingham, England, where, Roger says, "You could either escape through football or music. And I wasn't much good at football." His one interest is music and more music.

Nick Rhodes (born Nick Bates in 1962) has the best sense of humor of any of the fab five. Besides music, he loves photography. He also loves animals. Fans consider him, along with Simon

MTV's Martha Quinn, J. J. Jackson, and Nina Blackwood with Simon Le Bon of Duran Duran.

John Bellissimo

Duran Duran
Courtesy SONY Corporation of America

and John, one of the most attractive of the Durans. Think how dull videoland would be without Duran Duran's special magic. They've set the standard for beauty and careful work. If other artists are now making prettier or more spectacular videos, it's because Duran Duran showed them how.

To get in touch with Duran Duran write:

Capitol Records
1750 North Vine Street
Hollywood, CA 90028

EMI-UK Records, Ltd.
20 Manchester Square
London, WA 1ES
England

MADONNA

Madonna is one of the biggest stars of the new era of music video. In mid-1983 she was an unknown with little music background. Her first record had just been released. By the end of 1984 she was at the top of the charts. Her success was due mainly to a string of glossy videos, perfect showcases for this pretty and vivacious new star.

Madonna is her real name, or at least part of it. She was born Madonna Louise Ciccone to a large family (five brothers and two sisters) in the Detroit suburb of Bay City, Michigan. She appeared in plays in the three Catholic high schools she attended. She also took piano lessons and dance, where her real talent seemed to be. A ballet teacher helped her get a dance scholarship at the University of Michigan. But seventeen-year-old Madonna was impatient. She quit college and landed in New York City in 1978 with thirty-five dollars to her name. She worked briefly with a

Madonna
Steven Meisel, Album Cover, "Like a Virgin"

couple of the city's biggest dance troupes. Still, it wasn't what she wanted.

Madonna was now attracted to the glittering pop-music world. She learned to play some instruments and began appearing with a series of New York loft and garage bands. An audition got her a stint as a singer/dancer with a French disco star in Paris. It wasn't the road to stardom she had hoped for.

Back in New York she began writing, recording, and promoting her own material. It was hard work, but it landed her a record contract. Her first album, called simply *Madonna,* started slow. It began to catch on in clubs, then on black radio stations. It was the videos for such cuts as "Borderline" and "Holiday" that brought Madonna's voice, face, and figure to the attention of a mass audience. And they liked what they saw and what they heard. *Madonna* soared past platinum and is

Madonna
Steven Meisel

on its way to double platinum. That was unheard-of success for a debut album.

Like a Virgin, Madonna's second album, is even bigger. Not only is the record a chart buster, the video for the title song was the most popular on MTV as 1985 began.

Music-business professionals are keenly aware that this savvy new superstar made it to the top without ever having appeared in concert. A strong live act was once considered absolutely necessary for rock stardom. Videos have changed all that.

Will Madonna take her act on the road? Attractive and graceful, she seems sure to conquer that world as well. But, as usual, she's following her own instincts, not the advice of the "experts." At the moment she is more interested in films than concerts. Her first major role, in the film *Desperately Seeking Susan,* has attracted rave reviews and a large audience. The future for a performer of Madonna's talent and drive seems almost unlimited.

To contact Madonna write:

Sire Records
3 East 54th Street
New York, NY 10022

Warner Brothers Records
3300 Warner Boulevard
Burbank, CA 91510

VAN HALEN

If you want to start a band, the group you can learn the most from is Van Halen. They started young, worked hard, learned how to promote themselves, and never took themselves too seriously. They're the super party band of all time. Their style is sort of, but not really, heavy metal.

Alex Van Halen was born in Holland in 1955, his brother Eddie in 1957. Their father was a musician, and both boys studied piano. Alex and Eddie's parents expected them to become concert pianists when they grew up, and they received a strict classical training. When the Van Halen family moved to California in 1967, the boys discovered rock. After that they played the piano only because they had to. But Alex played the drums because he wanted to, and nobody could keep Eddie away from the guitar.

David Lee Roth, Van Halen's combination lead singer, comic, dancer, acrobat, and wildman, was born in 1955 in Bloomington, Indiana. David's

Alex Van Halen, David Lee Roth, Eddie Van Halen, and Michael Anthony

Courtesy Van Halen Productions

father is a wealthy doctor. The Roths settled in California when David was in high school. The same year David was born, Michael Anthony was born in Chicago. He came from a family of musicians. Besides playing trumpet in his high-school marching band, he took up the bass guitar. He, too, moved to California, where he met the Van Halen brothers at Pasadena City College. By then Alex and Eddie had formed a band called Mammoth and stolen the lead singer of a rival band, none other than David Lee Roth. When the guys got together, the chemistry was right for putting together one of the most popular rock bands in the world.

They called themselves Van Halen, which sometimes confuses people who don't know the group. They think David is Van Halen. Though David is a vital and exciting member of the group, there is probably no greater electric guitar player around these days than Eddie Van Halen. Musicians admire his new ways of playing lead guitar. Just listen to his steamy guitar solo on Michael Jackson's "Beat It." Many people think "Beat It" would never have been the hit it was if it hadn't been for Eddie Van Halen's sizzling sound. Eddie Van Halen's guitar playing was also a featured attraction on "Thriller."

When the Van Halen band was first formed, they played backyard parties for high-school kids, frat parties, and whatever clubs would hire them. Soon they were putting on their own outdoor concerts. Next they started renting halls, going to neighborhood high schools and record stores to drum up an audience. They'd charge a couple of dollars per kid and put on a sensational show. It wasn't long before their concerts were packed with fans.

They grabbed every chance that came their way to play, working a schedule that would have left most musicians too tired to move. It paid off. Van Halen became a regular opening act at a club on Sunset Strip in Hollywood. A mass of fans came to see them perform at the Pasadena Civic Auditorium. They began to hit it really big in the clubs, and that led to their real break, a chance to make a record for Warner Brothers.

Van Halen's strength is their honesty. Even though when they tour they have tons of equipment, that is one band that could entertain people playing on a street corner in their old jeans. They don't need fancy packaging. They don't need a lot of hype. When it came time to make a record, they didn't spend months making everything perfect. They just knocked out some good rock 'n' roll. The record went platinum and then some. Van Halen was a smash superstar band.

Hit records are only part of the Van Halen story. The band that had started out playing parties became the all-time party band on tour. Fans loved the lively, fun-filled concerts Van Halen put on. Often fans were invited to a Van Halen party after the concert.

Van Halen approached video the same way they approached their first record. The video featuring their hit song "Jump" was shot with one 16-mm handheld camera. The video cost six hundred dollars, which is a joke compared to what most videos cost. But Van Halen didn't need slick effects and multimillion-dollar directors and equipment. They only needed to be themselves, Van Halen, and that's what the video showed. MTV fans ate the video up. A later video, "Hot for Teacher," showed off the band's great sense of humor. Clowning around is a Van Halen specialty. The kids acting in the video seemed to be having almost as much fun as the band.

MTV paid tribute to Van Halen's popularity with video fans by sponsoring a "Lost Weekend with Van Halen" contest in 1984. Van Halen gave the winner the royal treatment, beginning with a cake thrown in his face by the band and crew. The follow-up treatment and prizes more than made up for the cake. David Lee Roth was at his party-host best, and when David's at his best nobody in rock is better.

Girls love to watch David, which is only fair because David spends a lot of time watching girls. Years of acrobatics have made him one of the most ruggedly built of all modern rock stars. He takes care of himself, too, to stay in shape and has often spoken out against taking drugs. Van Halen's bright good-time image has no dark side.

Maybe it's because Alex and Eddie Van Halen come from a musical family that they're so close to their parents. Maybe it's because they had an easier childhood than a lot of rock musicians. They didn't quit school, run away from home, or spend their teen years alone without friends. Eddie is married to actress Valerie Bertinelli. They make one of the cutest couples in show business. Michael Anthony is married to his high-school girlfriend.

If all this sounds too quiet for you, don't be fooled. Just play a Van Halen record, go to a Van Halen concert, or watch a Van Halen video, and you'll get all the excitement you need. Though Van Halen has grown up since the days they played at teen parties, they still have that party spirit. When they play they're happy. And so are their fans.

To get in touch with Van Halen write:

Warner Brothers Records
3300 Warner Boulevard
Burbank, CA 91510

Van Halen Productions
6525 Sunset Boulevard
North Hollywood, CA 91602

BOY GEORGE AND CULTURE CLUB

He's six feet tall, but he seems as sweet and friendly as a little kid. Some people think of him that way, as a little boy playing dress-up. Maybe that's why he looks right holding a Cabbage Patch doll. Maybe that's why he's been compared to a teddy bear. Teens like him. Grown-ups like him. Children like him. Though he wears colorful costumes and likes to look different, his songs and videos are never violent or scary. His originality and charm shine through despite or because of the way he dresses. So does his sense of humor.

For someone so extraordinary, Boy George's background is surprisingly ordinary. One of six children, Boy George was born in London in 1961. His real name is George O'Dowd. His father was a builder and a boxing coach, and

George was raised in a tough working-class neighborhood. Tough neighborhoods are hard places to grow up in, especially if you're sensitive and creative like George. George has an artist's eye for color and style. In order to escape the drabness of his neighborhood George moved to a more colorful part of London when he was fifteen.

To support himself George worked as a model, a printer, and a salesman and did makeup for the Royal Shakespeare Company, England's famous theater group. What he really loved, though, was dressing up in different styles of clothes and going to clubs to hear rock music. The outrageous way he dressed had already made people notice him in the world of rock clubs. In 1981 he became friends with Sue Clowes, now a famous fashion designer. Together they started a small clothing store called the Foundry. There George experimented boldly with different kinds of clothes. He wore what he wanted no matter what anybody else said. He dressed the way he thought he looked best.

If Boy George had wanted a career in fashion or design, he could have had one. But he was to find another route to fame. Singing with a band called Bow Wow Wow, he was spotted by bassist Mikey Craig, who asked him to help form a new band. Ex–Adam and the Ants drummer Jon Moss joined George and Mikey. Add guitarist Roy Hay

Culture Club's Boy George
Mark Weiss

and the new band was ready to take over the world.

But what to call themselves? The members of the band came from very different backgrounds. Hay was from a London suburb. Jon, who's Jewish, had grown up in a middle-class family. A good student, he could have gone to England's great Cambridge University if he'd wanted. Mikey is black. His family comes from the island of Jamaica in the West Indies. The group was familiar with many kinds of music: Motown soul, reggae, even American country. If the band had one message, it was tolerance. What better name than Culture Club, a club for people of every culture and belief?

Boy George's costumes reflected the band's point of view. At first he wore the same kinds of hats Orthodox Jewish rabbis do. His hair was braided into a dreadlock style to remind people of the Rastafarians of Jamaica. There were Hebrew letters on his clothes, and he wore a Christian cross. Recently he has appeared with a crew cut and glasses.

The band began writing songs, and in October 1981 they appeared in concert for the first time. It wasn't long before an English record-company executive noticed them and they made their first album. But it was their first single, "Do You Really Want to Hurt Me," which made Culture Club a big band in America.

Later albums like *Colour by Numbers* and *Waking Up with the House on Fire* were smash hits. Boy George was proving an appealing video draw as well. Despite the warm rhythms of Culture Club's music, there was a wistful side to the songs which Boy George brought out beautifully. He is a witty guest on talk shows, and his picture has appeared on the covers of magazines like *Newsweek* and *Rolling Stone*. Boy George look-alike contests are very popular. With Culture Club's videos getting ever more lavish and artistic, their records continue to roll gold and platinum.

Successful rock bands work hard. If there's one thing Boy George has been very outspoken about, it's the need for rock artists to lead healthy, disciplined lives. Boy George doesn't smoke, drinks very little, and hates all drugs. He doesn't believe in staying up late and doesn't often go to parties. He also believes that all kinds of people are beautiful, be they fat, short, tall, or skinny. If it were up to Boy George, everybody would smile and be kind to each other. Difference isn't necessarily weird or dangerous, and it's really okay to be gentle. That's the message of Culture Club.

To get in touch with Culture Club write:

Epic Records
1801 Century Park West
Los Angeles, CA 90067

Culture Club
c/o Zebra
P.O. Box 947
Hollywood, CA 90028

Wedge Music Ltd.
63 Gresvenor Street
London, WIX 9DA
England

MICHAEL JACKSON

If you went anywhere in the world and said the name Michael Jackson, people would know who you were talking about. They might not know who won an Academy Award this year. They might not know who was the top quarterback in the NFL. They might not know the name of the president of the United States or even the name of the president of their very own country. But from small villages to big cities scattered across the earth people have heard of Michael Jackson. Now, that's a superstar for you. Actually, that's more than being a superstar. That's being a megastar. Michael Jackson was a superstar who became a megastar thanks to videos.

Michael was born into a large family in Gary, Indiana, in 1958. Michael's parents loved music. His mother played clarinet and sang. His father played guitar and sang. For a while Mr. Jackson

Michael Jackson and his brothers on the Victory Tour.
John Bellissimo

was part of a band called the Falcons. Though Mr. Jackson worked for U.S. Steel, he had an eye for musical talent. He didn't have to look far. There was plenty right in his own family.

The Jackson kids began singing and playing instruments early. When Jackie, Tito, Jermaine, and Marlon decided to form a band together, they realized they needed a lead singer. It just so happened that when little Michael was only four years old he began learning how to dance and play the bongo. Next he tackled singing. A year later, Michael was ready to be the Jackson Five's lead singer. He wasn't just cute. He was good. By 1967 the group was well known in their hometown. They even made a couple of singles for a local record company.

Then came a big break. In 1969 the Jackson Five won the talent contest at the Apollo Theater in New York City's Harlem. You had to be special to please the audience at the Apollo Theater. They knew a lot about music. After the Apollo, people outside Gary began noticing the Jacksons. One of the people who noticed them was the legendary singer Diana Ross. Thanks in part to her, the Jackson Five got a contract with Motown Records. A year later, everybody in the band, including eleven-year-old-Michael, was a star.

In 1976, after fabulous tours and hit records, the group changed their name to the Jacksons and signed with Epic Records. Randy replaced Jermaine, who stayed with Motown. Michael showed his gift for dancing a couple of years later when he played the Scarecrow in the movie *The Wiz*. He also made a multiplatinum record, *Off the Wall,* and won the first of what would be a giant-sized collection of Grammy awards. More wonders followed. But they were all topped by the success of Michael's 1982 *Thriller* album. It was indeed a record-setting record.

The first hit song from *Thriller* to become a video was "Billie Jean." Michael moved like no-

The Victory Tour
John Bellissimo

body had ever moved in a video before. He danced like nobody had ever danced in a video before. His style was original. It was completely his own. His singing was super, too.

Then along came the video for "Beat It." Fans couldn't keep their eyes off the television screen when it came on. Suddenly videos didn't seem like promos anymore. They weren't merely a means of selling records. They didn't seem junky or second-rate anymore. Sad to say, a lot of rock videos had seemed confusing, cheaply made, and

41

thrown together. Michael Jackson gave videos class.

The *Thriller* video went even further. It was longer and told a fuller story than other videos. After *Thriller,* videos would never be the same. From now on they were a new art form. The rhythmic music, the exciting dancing, the wild makeup made *Thriller* appear to be a mini–monster-musical movie. The big news after Michael's video triumphs was the spectacular 1984 Victory tour sponsored by Pepsi-Cola.

By 1985 everybody from little kids to senior citizens could tell you all about Michael Jackson. He was the first black artist to become popular with white video fans, pioneering the way for other black performers. It seems the whole world knows that he lives in a huge house in California; that he's deeply religious and a vegetarian; that he has lots of pets, including a llama and a boa constrictor. He loves cartoons and movies, is very sweet, and is still as charming as he was when he was little Michael, lead singer with the Jackson Five.

But if you think all the talent in the Jackson family went to the boys, then you'd better think again. Michael has two musically gifted sisters, LaToya and Janet. When she was only seven, Janet joined her famous brothers onstage at the MGM Grand Hotel in Las Vegas. She pretended first that she was movie star Mae West, then that

Janet Jackson

Joe Jackson Productions, Inc., Courtesy A&M Records

she was singer Cher. The audience loved her. When she was ten, she played Penny Gordon on the television show *Good Times*. She has also been on *Different Strokes* and *Fame*.

Her very first A and M album, *Janet Jackson,* showed that she's a sparkling entertainer, as did her second album, *Dream Street*. She's beautiful, too, a natural for video. And, like the rest of her family, she's got the "Jackson magic."

To get in touch with Michael Jackson write:

Epic Records
51 West 52nd Street
New York, NY 10019

EURYTHMICS

She is tall, with close-cropped orange hair and outlandish clothes. He is short, wears glasses, usually dark, and has hair that looks as if it hasn't been combed in months. They are Annie Lennox and Dave Stewart, Eurythmics. Not *the* Eurythmics, just Eurythmics. The name tells you something about them.

Eurythmics is a practice first developed in the nineteenth century which combines dance movement and music. Annie studied eurythmy while she was at High School for Girls in her native Scotland. Annie is an accomplished flautist—she plays the flute. She also plays the piano, harpsichord, and harmonium (a type of organ).

Annie was born in the North Sea city of Aberdeen on Christmas Day 1954. Her family was strictly working-class, but her musical talent won her a scholarship to the high-class High School for Girls, and upon graduation to the even more prestigious Royal Academy of Music in London.

44

Eurythmics
Courtesy RCA Records

Annie hated the Royal Academy; the atmosphere was stifling. Though she liked and still likes classical music, she found herself more attracted to the music of David Bowie and Stevie Wonder. After what Annie calls "three dreadful years," she quit the academy. But she was in for another "three dreadful years" trying to get along in the tough London music world, and getting nowhere.

In the spring of 1977 Annie was waitressing in a health-food restaurant when she met Dave Stewart. "He looked like he'd been dragged through a hedge backward."

Dave was born in 1952 in Sunderland, a town in the north of England. He'd been a fanatic soccer player until, at the age of twelve, he broke his knee and was laid up for a long period. In the hospital he was given a guitar to amuse himself, and he developed a new obsession, music. Two years later he tried to run away with the band at the first rock concert he saw. They sent him home; but, undaunted, he came back during the next school vacation and followed the tour. He was even able to talk himself into being the opening act and was popular because he looked so young and cute.

Success, however, was not assured. For the next few years Dave lived a chaotic life, experimenting with all different types of music, from medieval to blues, folk, and funk. He joined a variety of groups and when all else failed did odd jobs.

His meeting with Annie was not chance. A friend told him about this girl with a remarkable voice who was working as a waitress. That night Dave and his friend went back to Annie's apartment and listened to her play the harmonium that she had somehow crammed into her tiny room and sing complicated songs. "She sat there like the Phantom of the Opera," Dave recalls.

Annie and Dave joined with songwriter/guitarist Peet Coombes to form the Tourists. The group had some success, a lot of hard times, and finally broke up. On their own, Annie and Dave began creating what was to become Eurythmics music. The first Eurythmics album, *In the Garden,* was recorded in 1980 in Germany. Some rock critics praised it, but it didn't sell.

With this commercial flop Annie and Dave hit rock bottom. Annie recalls she spent a lot of time crying. Dave wound up in the hospital requiring major surgery to correct injuries suffered in an auto accident years before.

The strains of that time ended the romantic relationship between Annie and Dave, but not the professional relationship. Depressed, Annie took off for Aberdeen and home. One night she got a call from Dave, who played some new songs for her over the phone. She was enthusiastic and rushed back to London. They managed to borrow enough money to buy a cheap tape machine and recorded most of the tracks of *Sweet Dreams (Are Made of This)* in a warehouse. The recordings, meant only as demos, were released practically as is. The album cost about seven hundred dollars to make. It is probably the most cheaply produced album ever to hit the Top 40.

Sweet Dreams (Are Made of This) was a huge, and unexpected, success. Eurythmics are also dynamite onstage. But it was the videos that made them superstars. Unlike many performers, who use outside directors, Annie and Dave direct their own videos. Eurythmics' videos are filled with strange and striking images. Most striking of all is Annie's dramatic and ever-changing appearance. In the "Sweet Dreams" video the TV-watching public got a good look at Annie's orange crew cut. In "Love Is a Stranger" she wears a lot of wigs and disguises. She showed up at the 1983 Grammy awards dressed like Elvis Presley, wig and all. Part of the fascination of Eurythmics is seeing what Annie is going to look like this time.

Though the road has been hard, the future for Eurythmics looks bright. They have total control of their work. They write their own music and record it in a sixteenth-century London church, which they own. They can produce albums and videos without unusual fuss, expense, or interference. "When we work," says Annie, "we're able to close the door from all other entrances that want to pressure us. We just take our time and look for what we find exciting. . . .

"Creativity," she says, "is an ongoing process." To get in touch with Eurythmics write:

Eurythmics Fan Club
P.O. Box 245
London N89 QG
England

RCA Records
1133 Avenue of the Americas
New York, NY 10036

PAT BENATAR

She's rock music's top female star. Her records go platinum. Her career is dotted with Grammy awards. She's made many videos, and fans keep clamoring for more. For several years girls in high school have copied the Pat Benatar look. But don't be fooled by the leather and spandex she wore when she launched her career. That's a costume. If there's one word that best describes Pat Benatar, the word is *real*.

She was born Pat Andrzejewski in Brooklyn, New York, in 1953 and grew up on Long Island. Pat came by her love of music naturally, because her mother had been an opera singer. Pat's mother encouraged her to study opera, too, so Pat took voice lessons. As any Benatar fan will tell you, she has a terrific voice. Thanks to the lessons, she also knows how to take care of her voice.

Pat Benatar
Matthew Rolston

When Pat was born, her mother quit opera to take care of her. Pat's father worked in a sheet-metal factory. But money was scarce, so Pat's mother went to work. It was too late for Pat's mother to return to opera, and she wound up working first as a beautician and then as a teller in a bank. Pat was to have her chance at opera, too, when at seventeen she went to New York City's famous Juilliard School of Music.

But opera was Pat's mother's dream. Pat's was rock, and she quit Juilliard. For a while it looked as if Pat might repeat her mother's story and quit music altogether. At nineteen the biggest thing in her life wasn't music. It was getting married to a guy named Dennis Benatar. Pat and Dennis went to live on an army base in Virginia, and Pat got a job as a teller in a bank. But a bank job just wasn't for her, and soon she was singing again.

Part of what makes Pat Benatar so likable is her honesty. Part of what makes her seem so real is that she doesn't brag. Some superstars say they always knew they would become famous artists. Not Pat. She admits she never expected such a fantastic thing to happen. She'd always thought of herself as "the skinny kid with the big teeth." In the world of rock, where egos grow as big as the moon, Pat's way of poking fun at herself is refreshing. Actually, she's a strikingly good-looking, dark-eyed, five-foot-two dynamite performer. In concert she's pure energy.

Pat's career began to take off when she returned to New York in 1975. Like most singers no matter how talented, she struggled to find the style that was right for her. At last she came up with her own hard-rock sound. Her big break came when she sang at Catch a Rising Star, a New York club where many terrific artists have got their start. The club's owner liked Pat's singing so much he became her manager. When he landed her a recording contract with Chrysalis Records, Pat's star began to rise, all right—and fast.

In 1981 a lead guitarist from Cleveland, Ohio, joined Pat's band. His name was Neil Geraldo. By that time Pat was no longer married to Dennis Benatar, and in 1982 she married Neil. Though Pat works very hard at her music, work isn't her whole life. Being a wife and mother as well as a singer means a lot to her. Part of being real is knowing that family is an important part of life.

When she sings, Pat demands the best from herself and everyone around her. There are artists whose concerts aren't very interesting but who make good records, or artists who can only make videos but who on tour and on records are disappointing. Pat never disappoints. Not only is she too talented to let that happen, she could never be so lazy or careless. Her records are super, and she's super on tour. Then there are artists who don't make good videos. Pat's videos are first-rate. She makes sure they're exactly right before she allows them to be released.

Take a standout video like "Love Is a Battlefield." The amount of work that went into this storytelling video is amazing. The work shows. Take a look at how well Pat dances in the video. A lot of stars would quit work when they were pregnant, but not Pat. She went right on making videos, including the ultrapopular, beautiful "We Belong Together" and the adorable "The Ooh Ooh Song."

If you watch Pat's new videos, you can see

Pat Benatar
Wayne Masser

how her image is changing. She is stronger and more mature. All kinds of people like her now, grown-ups as well as kids. That's rare in rock. But then, Pat is rare. She's a rock star who lives quietly in California and doesn't flaunt her wealth. She's a rock star with opera training. She's a rock star with more than music in her life.

Pat Benatar is the kind of woman most girls would like to be when they grow up. That's what it means to be real.

To get in touch with Pat Benatar write:

Chrysalis Records
9255 Sunset Boulevard
Los Angeles, CA 90069

DAVID BOWIE

He's been the major force in rock music for years. He may even be the most original and influential single artist rock music has ever known. If you think that's strong praise, remember David Bowie cut his first record when he was a teenager. That was over twenty years ago. Today he's still daring, new, and exciting. Unlike other legendary figures in rock, Bowie isn't living off a reputation made in the past. He doesn't sing the way he used to. He doesn't write the same kinds of songs. No, Bowie is a legend not only because of what he did yesterday, but because of what he's doing now and what he'll do tomorrow. From Billy Idol to Duran Duran, most young rock stars admit they owe a lot to David Bowie.

He was born David Robert Jones in London in 1947. He began playing the saxophone at the age of twelve, later moving on to the guitar. Even at twelve Bowie was bold. All on his own he looked up the phone number of a well-known sax player in the London phone book and asked to take lessons! Being adventurous and taking risks were part of Bowie then and are part of Bowie now.

In high school Bowie played in a band called George and the Dragons. It was in high school, too, that he almost went blind. During a fight he was hit in the eye and the pupil of his left eye was paralyzed. That only made Bowie's already unusual eyes (one is blue and one gray) even more unusual.

At school Bowie excelled at sports and at art but not at his studies. When he left school he tried working as a commercial artist. But soon he was back at his music, playing with different bands. The King Bees, the Mannish Boys, and the Lower Thirds were three of the groups. Along the way the name David Jones was dropped and the young rock performer became David Bowie. He didn't want to be confused with another David Jones, who was with the rock band the Monkees. The name Bowie comes from the Bowie knife that was used on the American frontier.

One thing that makes David Bowie different from a lot of other artists is his need to withdraw from music for long stretches of time and devote himself to other interests. Back in the sixties, after cutting a successful single record he turned away from rock and became involved in acting, mime, and film. He also delved deeply into Bud-

David Bowie
Greg Gorman, 1984

dhism, practically becoming a Buddhist monk.
But in 1969 a song about Major Tom, an astronaut
lost in space, called "Space Oddity" proved that
Bowie was still a great musical talent. The only
reason he'd made the record was to find the
money to organize a theater group.

For a long time Bowie had been a cult figure
admired by the kind of serious rock fan who
doesn't care if an artist is a superstar or not. What
counts with this kind of fan is how imaginative an
artist is, how creative. Bowie is so good that he

was able to hold on to these choosy fans even as his fame grew. His fame was growing like crazy because he was shaking up rock and changing it to the core.

In 1971 came the hit song "Changes" from his *Hunky Dory* album. In 1972 Bowie launched a new trend in music called glitter rock when his album *The Rise and Fall of Ziggy Stardust and the Spiders from Mars* was released. The character Ziggy was an invention of Bowie's, and he went on tour playing the role of the dazzling Ziggy. The tour was as much a spectacular show as a concert, a wild fantasy with Bowie's hair dyed orange. He wore glittering costumes and platform shoes. Fans had never seen a concert quite like it before. But then, Bowie is as much an actor as a singer.

If there were still any lingering doubts about his acting ability, the 1976 sci-fi movie starring Bowie called *The Man Who Fell to Earth* put them to rest. By then Bowie had abandoned Ziggy. Inventing new styles and leaving them behind just when they're catching on is typical of Bowie.

While other artists were involved in punk Bowie found a new challenge in electronic music, synthesizers. He was first, but synthesizer bands would soon become the rage in rock. Bowie surprised people with his *Young Americans* album, a tribute to soul. It won him a black audience. He was delighted to be one of the first white performers to appear on the *Soul Train* television show. One of Bowie's best songs, "Fame" (written with the great John Lennon of the Beatles), was on this album.

Bowie entered his Thin White Duke phase when he went on tour to promote his *Station to Station* album. Bowie's tours have always been triumphs. Take his 1983 Serious Moonlight tour, one of the biggest successes in rock history.

In 1980 Bowie starred in a major play on Broadway, *The Elephant Man.* He added to his screen credits when he appeared in a horror movie called *The Hunger.* Critics admired the dignified way he played a character who grew old in just a few hours' time. *Merry Christmas, Mr. Lawrence* is a Bowie film about British soldiers in a Japanese prison camp during World War II. Bowie has made cameo appearances in other recent films and has done the music for still others.

David Bowie's genius spilled over into video early, beginning with his use of concert clips. Video captured his imagination. He knew it was an art form that would transform music. As usual, Bowie had his mind on the future. The video "Fashion," from Bowie's 1980 album *Scary Monsters,* emphasizes dance and movement. Alan Hunter, not yet an MTV VJ, appeared briefly in the video. Watch for him when you see it. More innovative videos, such as "Ashes to Ashes," fol-

Scene for David Bowie's "Jazzin' for Blue Jean."
Courtesy SONY Corporation Of America

lowed. This one influenced a lot of artists who were looking to Bowie's videos for ideas.

As the videos continued to flow three of the most popular, "China Girl," "Let's Dance," and "Modern Love," were brought out on video cassette by Sony Video 45. "Jazzin' for Blue Jean," Bowie's twenty-minute minimovie-type video, is also available on Sony Video 45. Though there is a shorter version of the video, it's the longer one which is most interesting. The longer format allows a story to be told in depth, and Bowie gets to play two roles, one ordinary and one extraordinary.

Who knows, perhaps one of these days he'll play triplets. The amazing David Bowie just keeps going on and on blazing new trails. Well, what can you expect of a man independent and daring enough to name his only son Zowie Bowie? With his talent and sense of showmanship David Bowie will remain a giant on the rock scene as long as he wants.

To get in touch with David Bowie write:

EMI-America Records
6920 Sunset Boulevard
Los Angeles, CA 90028

HALL AND OATES

Daryl Hall is tall and has blond hair. John Oates is short and has dark hair. They may look like opposites, but when it comes to rock music they're dynamite together. There's never been a duo as popular as Hall and Oates in the history of rock. Why? Well, the answer's very simple. They're wonderful musicians and super songwriters.

Granted, Hall and Oates have charm. Daryl Hall especially sets teenage girls sighing. The two guys manage to be attractive without wearing ruffled shirts and fancy clothes, or getting their hair cut in some outrageous way. Hall and Oates would consider that sort of thing phony. They've always been straightforward creative musicians, and that's the only thing they want to be known for.

Videowise, they're exciting and energetic performers. MTV understood this right from the

Hall & Oates

Photograph by Jean Pagliuso, Courtesy The Press Office, Ltd.

start. Hall and Oates have been popular guest VJs on MTV. MTV has done documentaries on the pair. MTV helped sponsor their Big Bam Boom tour. Hall and Oates have also appeared in concert on HBO (Home Box Office). Part of the reason for all the television attention is that Hall and Oates have fans in every age group. Kids like them, but so do adults. Girls like them, but so do boys. Their New York City–inspired music mixes black and white sound. When it comes to rock and soul, nobody's better than Hall and Oates. No wonder their fans come from so many backgrounds and so many places.

Hall and Oates first met in Philadelphia, Pennsylvania, in the late 1960s. Oates was studying journalism at Temple University while Hall was studying music. Both played in separate bands. First they became friends, then roommates. Knowing each other before they became professionals made a big difference later. Friendship gave them a solid base from which to launch a career.

Somewhere along the line Oates gave up journalism for music. Somewhere along the line Hall joined a band called Gulliver. Oates sometimes played with it, too. Hall and Oates discovered just how well they worked together. They decided to leave the band and perform as a duo. Their talent won them a small but devoted following of fans who knew good music when they heard it.

In 1972 their first album, *Whole Oats,* was released. They started winning major attention with their next album, *Abandoned Luncheonette.* In 1974 they had a hit song, "She's Gone." The duo was moving up and in on the music world. More hits followed, like "Rich Girl," which reached number one on the charts. But it was the album *Voices* in 1980 that really put Hall and Oates solidly on top. The duo produced the album themselves, and it was so original it spread like wildfire among rock fans. After that it was platinum and gold. Hall and Oates found success not only on the pop chart but on R & B and dance charts as well.

Daryl Hall

Photograph by Jean Pagliuso, Courtesy The Press Office, Ltd.

Glittering special effects can never take the place of talent, and on tour Hall and Oates dazzle in concert mainly because they are such good musicians. The same is true of their videos. Watch any Hall and Oates video closely and you'll see that the focus of their videos is always Hall and Oates themselves.

Some artists seem to get lost in their own videos. Images of dancers, scenery, color, you name it, take over, and the next thing you know the artists are shoved into the background. That never happens with Hall and Oates. They don't make busy videos. They make good videos, and the reason they're good is that Hall and Oates are such talented performers.

John Oates
Photograph by Jean Pagliuso, Courtesy The Press Office, Ltd.

Though they're always moving ahead crea-
tively, their music rings with the best sounds of
the fifties and early sixties. That's because they
love and understand the music of that time themselves. And when it comes to music, Hall and
Oates do what they please. Luckily, it pleases the
rest of us, too.

To get in touch with Hall and Oates write:

RCA Records
1133 Avenue of the Americas
New York, NY 10036

Whole Oats Enterprises
130 West 57th Street
New York, NY 10019

PRINCE

Put curls, ruffles, dazzling showmanship, the color purple for royalty, and one wild guitar together, and you've got Prince. He's a musical whiz who plays a whole band's worth of instruments. He's a movie star whose 1984 video-style film *Purple Rain* was a sensational supersmash. People went to see it in movie theaters in record numbers, and they bought it on video cassette in record numbers, too. He won and shared a total of three 1984 Grammy Awards, and an Academy Award.

Prince has been compared to music greats like Elvis Presley and Jimi Hendrix. He's been compared to movie great Marlon Brando. What Bruce Springsteen is to New Jersey and Billy Joel is to Long Island, Prince is to his hometown, Minneapolis, Minnesota. He's the local kid who made it really big in the big time but who still cares an awful lot about home.

Prince
John Bellissimo

Prince Rogers Nelson was born in Minneapolis in 1958. He was named after the Prince Rogers Band, his father's jazz combo; his mother was a singer. Not surprisingly, Prince learned to play the piano as a child. By the time he was in junior high school he had formed a band called Champagne, which played high-school dances. These days when he performs with his band it's Prince and the Revolution.

When Prince was a teenager he went to New York hoping for a record contract. He didn't get one, partly because he wouldn't let anyone else produce his record. He wanted to make the major decisions about his own work himself. Talk about having faith in yourself! Most teenagers would have been thankful to take anything a record company offered them. Contracts aren't easy to get.

When Prince found out that most record companies thought he was too young to have the kind of control he wanted, he went to California, where Warner Brothers gave him the kind of contract he wanted. This just proves that Prince was more than a musical prodigy. He had a knack for business which went way beyond his years.

Prince's first album was released in 1978. By 1982, when Prince's very popular double album was released, he was a famous songwriter, singer, and musician. He was at his best on tour. Part of the appeal of *Purple Rain* is that it's like one sensational rock concert. Movie tickets are cheaper than concert tickets, so the movie was a double treat for rock fans.

Prince is one of the most independent of rock stars. He hates to be interviewed. Some people say he's moody. Some people say he's hard to get to know. But everybody says he's got talent, and everybody respects him for all he's achieved. Prince isn't just a prince. He's the king of the rock.

To get in touch with Prince write:

Warner Brothers Records,
3300 Warner Boulevard
Burbank, CA 91510

STING AND
THE POLICE

The Police have done it all. Sting, Stewart Copeland, and Andy Summers have been an enormously successful band for years. They have had hit singles, gold and platinum albums, sold-out world tours. They have been called the most important rock 'n' roll band since the Beatles.

As a video band, they're tops. *The Rolling Stone Book of Rock Video* says of the Police video for "Every Breath You Take": "Maybe the most outstanding enhanced-performance video ever, perfectly complementing the mood and pace of a classic song with immaculate video-sculpture setups, atmospheric lighting, slow dissolve edits, and lingering superimpositions. . . . Any way you slice it, it's an exceptional piece." You can't give much higher praise than that.

The Police have been able to stay out of the public eye for a couple of years, and then come back with a winner. In the frantic and ever-shifting rock 'n' roll world, that's rare.

The Police was formed by drummer Stewart Copeland, an American living in London, in early 1977. He was trying to put together a three-piece band. He wanted something simple, musically and commercially. Copeland thought a lot of bands had been destroyed by getting too big and expensive.

Vocalist, bass player, and occasional school-teacher Sting was the next recruit. He real name was Gordon Sumner. He picked up the nickname

The Police
Courtesy A&M Records

because he wore a yellow- and black-striped rugby jersey. It made him look like a bee, and he was first called Stinger. The final member of the band was Andy Summers, a guitarist who had worked with a number of other bands.

The group was not an overnight success. An early tour in America was a near disaster. Sting recalls: "In Poughkeepsie we played the Last Chance Saloon to a bartender and two other people. It was football night and everyone was home. It was a little embarrassing. . . . So we walked over, introduced ourselves, then went back to the stage and did our show. . . . It was a lesson. No matter how many people there are, give it all you've got."

From such a modest start the Police rose to the top. Now there are signs that the group may be splitting up.

The three members of the Police have been pursuing independent careers. But it's Sting who is the unquestioned star of this star group. If Copeland and Summers resent this, they aren't saying.

Sting realizes that a career as a rock superstar won't last forever. He says he does not want to fall prey to the "rock 'n' roll myth" and he's looking to the future. While he still enjoys playing rock, he candidly admits that he doesn't like listening to it. "My favorite music is Beethoven, Ravel, even Prokofiev."

It's the movies that have attracted Sting's attention. He had a small role in the multimillion-dollar sci-fi film *Dune*. The film bombed, but Sting's performance got raves. He plays the part of Dr. Frankenstein in a remake of *The Bride of Frankenstein*. A far more important step is a major role in the movie *Plenty*, costarring with Academy Award winner Meryl Streep.

A film producer who has worked with Sting has summed him up this way: "He's got this incredible, instinctual appeal. He's not what you would expect from a rock star. He's articulate and terribly, terribly bright."

To contact the Police write:

A & M Records
1416 North La Brea Avenue
Hollywood, CA 90028

TWISTED SISTER

Dee Snider, Twisted Sister's lead singer, described the band's early days: "We went onstage wearing dresses, lingerie, anything to get a reaction. We *thrive* on reaction. . . . At our first gig, we were playing to something like twenty-five people. After the first number, twenty of 'em walked out, and five tough-looking bikers stayed behind. They said, 'You guys have got real guts to come out here dressed like that.'"

"Basically," says Dee, "we're just a bunch of dirtbags."

Actually, unlike many rock stars who grew up in poverty and dropped out of high school, the members of Twisted grew up mainly in middle-class homes in the New York area. Some of them went to college, and Dee actually had classical voice training. He still uses the services of voice coach Katie Agresta, who has another famous student—Cyndi Lauper.

A.J. Pero, Jay Jay French, Dee Snider, Mark Mendoza, and Eddie Ojeda, members of Twisted Sister.

Mark Weiss

"I don't know how they sing every night," says Agresta. "Dee Snider is the perfect example. He's been my student for five years. We worked all that time to get him so that he could go out and scream every night and not lose his voice."

Twisted built a loyal following in the New York area. "We were packing the clubs," says Dee, "but recording companies refused to recognize us. We also opened for many big bands when they played the New York area, but it got to the point where no one would allow us to play with them for fear of being blown off the stage."

In 1982 Twisted went to England and got the kind of recognition it had never received in the

U.S. The band's wild live performance on British television led to a worldwide recording contract. Twisted became one of the top heavy-metal bands, first in Britain and then in the U.S.

It was TV once again, this time in the form of rock videos, that expanded the band's popularity beyond the circle of heavy-metal fans. Slick and hilarious videos of "We're Not Gonna Take It" and "I Wanna Rock" blasted their way to the top of rock-video popularity in 1984.

Dee says, "Either dig it or get out. It's all or nothing. People either love us or they hate us." But Twisted is finding that even those who are not great fans of heavy metal still find Twisted one of the most entertaining groups around.

To get in touch with Twisted Sister write:

Atlantic Records
75 Rockefeller Plaza
New York, NY 10020

THE CARS

They're an ill-assorted bunch. They range in size from the extremely tall, painfully thin Rick Ocasek to the diminutive Greg Hawkes. Of the group only Benjamin Orr can be considered handsome. But the Cars emphasize their individuality and oddness. Way back in the seventies the group shrewdly realized that how a band looked might be as important as how it sounded. They may be funny-looking, but they are also extremely smart. Early on they recognized how important videos were to become.

It's not that there is anything wrong with the Cars' music. Their sound is as distinctive and individual as their appearance. "All our albums sound like the Cars," Ocasek says. "And the Cars don't sound like any other band. When you hear them on the radio you can't mistake them for someone else." Their sound is cool and distant.

The Cars have been at or near the top since they released their first album in 1978. Most of

Ben Orr, David Robinson, Ric Ocasek, Elliot Easton and
Greg Hawkes of The Cars.

E. J. Camp/1984, Elektra, Courtesy Lookout Management

their albums have gone platinum or double
platinum.

To promote their records the Cars have turned
out a string of consistently good videos, and one
that is sure to be regarded as a classic, "You
Might Think." This is the comic gem in which
Ocasek in a variety of cartoon forms, from King
Kong to a fly, chases down the girl he loves.

Will success spoil the Cars? Have they settled
into a rut? As we said, the Cars are smart. They
know success can be a problem. Says Ocasek:

Ric Ocasek of The Cars
George Holz/1984, Elektra, Courtesy Lookout Management

"You do get jaded when you start learning what this business really means, what the people who work in it really think of it. It's hard to feel like an artist.

"At some points, you just feel like you can't come up with it anymore. What's it all for? Then you get revitalized and you conjure up that excitement again. You ask yourself, 'What am I doing this for? So I can go out and play in front of sixty thousand people instead of thirty thousand? Is it to make the record go to number two instead of number three?' I just want to make better records."

Hawkes says that members of the group do a lot of solo projects. "Solo projects are necessary for this group. Working with the same people for five years, you do get an urge to do something on your own. When you do come back you've had time to build up enthusiasm for the band again."

Some of Ocasek's outside projects involve producing and promoting the work of new and different bands. He also hopes to start his own record label to give local bands a start.

So the Cars may look funny, and do funny songs and videos. But they are dead serious about the future of rock music.

To contact the Cars write:

Elektra Records
665 Fifth Avenue
New York, NY 10022

79

BILLY IDOL

There are a lot of contradictions about Billy Idol. He looks like the perfect image of Britain's sneering, leather-clad, angry young punk rocker. And that's what he was—once. But he lives in New York, and has for years. While he was born in Britain, he spent some of his early years growing up on Long Island. And his songs are not just angry. Billy Idol writes and sings music you can dance to.

He was born William Broad. He took the name Idol as a joke. He is now well on his way to making that joke a reality. Billy entered the London rock scene in the mid-seventies. That was when punk rock was really taking hold. He started as a guitar player, but joined a group called Generation X (later shortened to Gen. X) as vocalist and front man.

Gen. X was highly regarded as one of the best of the new wave bands. By that time punk, or at

Billy Idol
© Tannenbaum-Sygma

least part of it, was being called new wave. In rock, labels pass in and out of fashion very quickly. One moment it's punk, the next it's new wave. The labels don't mean too much, and most artists like Billy Idol hate them.

Gen. X had some success, but after about four years and lots of personnel changes the group finally broke up. Billy wanted to pursue a solo career. The final song he made with Gen. X was "Dancing with Myself." That was also to be his first big solo hit.

The London music scene was being swept by another movement, this one called the new romanticism. It was all cool and unemotional synthesizer music, not at all Billy Idol's style. So he took off for New York in early 1981. When he arrived he found he already had a U.S. audience. In New York clubs people were actually dancing to "Dancing with Myself."

Billy's movie-star good looks and dramatic performing style made him a natural for videos. And coming from England he knew how important videos could be in building a career. His first video, "White Wedding," was a smash. And he had bigger things in mind. To make a video for "Dancing with Myself" Billy used director Tobe Hopper, who made the film *Poltergeist.*

The video is a spectacular effort. It features zombies and a bombed-out city. Says MTV's *Who's Who in Rock Video:* "Post-nuclear angst, brutal energy, terrifying violence, the collapse of civilization, and a good beat you can dance to— what else do you need?"

What else indeed. Idol has made the new medium his own. "I don't know if I'd call videos art," he says, "but I do see them as much more than promotion."

To contact Billy Idol write:

Chrysalis Records
9255 Sunset Boulevard
Los Angeles, CA 90069

"WEIRD AL" YANKOVIC

There can be some argument over who the king of rock video is. There's no argument at all about the number one funnyman: it's "Weird Al" Yankovic. In mid-1984 "Eat It"—"Weird Al's" hilarious parody of Michael Jackson's "Beat It"—was one of the most popular videos in the country. Weird Al says he wrote "Eat It" "to give Michael a little exposure and make him some money so he could buy his other glove."

Actually, Michael approved the parody and got a cut of the profits. Some performers won't let "Weird Al" mangle their music, but most seem to enjoy it and, in fact, are flattered by it. He turned Joan Jett's "I Love Rock 'n' Roll" into an ode to ice cream called "I Love Rocky Road." Greg Kihn's "Our Love in Jeopardy" became "I Lost on Jeopardy," a tribute to the world's most famous game show. His first video hit was "Ricky,"

"Weird Al" Yankovic
Jay Pope/CBS

a send-up not only of Toni Basil's "Mickey" but of the old Lucille Ball/Desi Arnaz show.

"Weird Al" was born in a middle-class suburb of Los Angeles in 1959. When he was seven his parents gave him an accordion. He thinks it was because the top polka artist at that time was Frank Yankovic—same name but no relation. He played at a few weddings, but there wasn't much call for a rock-'n'-roll accordionist.

As a teenager he began writing and recording musical parodies at home and sending them to the offbeat national radio personality Dr. Demento. "Weird Al" became a Demento favorite with his 1979 recording of "My Bologna," a pointed parody of the Knack's "My Sharona." Weird Al recorded it in a bathroom at California Polytechnic State University, where he was an architecture student. Later, he received his degree from the school.

In 1980 "Weird Al" recorded "Another One Rides the Bus," his parody of Queen's "Another One Bites the Dust." It became the most requested song in Demento's history, and a single began hitting the charts. "Weird Al" is grateful to Demento. "I guess you could call him my Dementor. I really owe it all to him."

"Weird Al" began appearing on shows like *The Today Show* and Entertainment Tonight, and doing concert appearances. But it was his video parodies that made him a national star.

So far he has been known mainly for his parodies, and some people think he may be just a novelty act. But "Weird Al" also does original comedy that is just as funny as his parodies. He wrote and arranged songs for the movie *Johnny Dangerously,* and his music got better reviews than the film itself.

Will he ever do serious songs? "I can't," he explains. "Whatever I write always ends up warped."

To get in touch with "Weird Al" Yankovic write:

Imaginary Entertainment
925 Westmount Drive
Los Angeles, CA 90069

THE GO-GO'S

It's tough for girls in rock 'n' roll. It's particularly tough for girls in bands. So the all-women Go-Go's are real pioneers. Not only have their records been successful, they have made some irrepressible videos as well.

When the group first started in 1977, most of the members had little performing experience. They improved rapidly, and by 1978 the Go-Go's were opening some big shows and playing regularly on the Los Angeles club circuit.

Still, the band had a lot of trouble getting U.S. record companies to take them seriously. They recorded their first single for a British company. Hardly anyone seemed to notice. Then they did a video, and the career of the Go-Go's began to turn around.

The video got them a record contract with the ominous-sounding IRS. It doesn't mean Internal Revenue Service; it means International Record

Kathy Valentine, Charlotte Caffey, Jane Wiedlin, Belinda Carlisle, Gina Schock of The Go-Go's.
Courtesy IRS Records

Syndicate. The single "Our Lips Are Sealed" from the debut album proved to be very popular, and an energetic and entertaining video helped to push sales along. The Go-Go's toured extensively. Finally the album *Beauty and the Beat* went on to sell more than two million copies. The Go-Go's became the first all-female band who wrote and performed their own material to reach the number one spot on the album charts. Other successes followed. The Go-Go's have proved that they are not just an oddity.

"We've always looked at ourselves more as a rock-'n'-roll act than just a 'girl group,'" says Belinda Carlisle, the lead vocalist. "Sure the Go Go's are lighthearted, but we have a serious side. . . ."

Bass guitarist Kathy Valentine adds, "It's no big deal to have an all-girl band anymore."

Late in 1984 the Go-Go's announced that Jane Wiedlin, one of the group's founding members, was leaving the band to pursue a solo career. The group itself, however, has no intention of breaking up. They are planning future records, tours, and of course videos.

To contact the Go-Go's write:

IRS
1416 North La Brea Avenue
Los Angeles, CA 90028

MEN AT WORK

Australia used to be the place where Britain sent its criminals. It was famous for kangaroos, koala bears, and sheep ranches. But recently the rest of the world has come to realize that there is a lot more than sheep raising going on down under. Australian movies and television shows have become very popular in Britain and the U.S. And Australian rock has hit the charts in a big way.

The success of Australian rock is due largely to the band called Men at Work. The band was formed in 1979. For a couple of years they worked what's known as the pub-and-club circuit in Melbourne. Sometimes they only made expenses. Often they didn't even make that much. Finally, in 1981, the group got a contract with the Australian branch of Columbia records. Their debut song was "Who Can It Be Now."

In 1981 videos were a lot more familiar in Australia than in the U.S. Most Australian groups did videos to promote their songs. Men at Work was

Men At Work
Courtesy Columbia Records

no different. Their video for "Who Can It Be Now" was strange, funny, and very popular. The video reached the U.S. about the time MTV was getting started. It was a smash on the new network. The popularity of the video pushed the sales of records for this previously unknown Australian group right to the top of the charts. Men at Work is one of the groups that can link its success directly to videos.

Other videos followed. They've all contained the group's characteristic crazy humor. Even a video like "It's a Mistake," which is about nuclear war, is funny. Sometimes humor is the best way to get a serious point across.

American fans got their first chance to see Men at Work in person during their summer 1983 tour. The tour proved that the group is just as good live as it is in videos.

To contact Men at Work write:

CBS/Columbia Records
51 West 52nd Street
New York, NY 10019

QUIET RIOT

They are among the jolliest of the heavy-metal bands. And their appeal reaches well beyond the usual circle of boy-biker metal enthusiasts. They are, of course, Quiet Riot.

A good part of the band's popularity is due to its skillful use of videos. Videos like "Cum On Feel the Noize" and "Party All Night" can set even traditional metal-haters smiling and clapping. With Quiet Riot the tongue is usually firmly in the cheek.

Quiet Riot, or what lead singer Kevin DuBrow called "the old Quiet Riot," was first formed back in 1975. The group became very popular in the Los Angeles area but was never able to secure a U.S. record contract. Frustrated, they broke up in 1980. DuBrow re-formed the group with Rudy Sarzo, Frankie Banali, and Carlos Cavazo early in 1982. The new Quiet Riot got a record con-

Rudy Sarzo, Frankie Banali, Kevin DuBrow, and Carlos Cavazo of Quiet Riot.

© Quite Right, Ltd., 1984, Photography by Aaron Rappaport

tract, and their first album, *Metal Health,* was the highest-charting heavy-metal debut in history. The single "Cum On Feel the Noize" made the top five, a real rarity for a heavy-metal record.

This success has given the band the confidence to bend, though not break, the heavy-metal formula. "People think heavy metal is all leather and studs, but I think it's in the vibe of the music," says Kevin. "The old Quiet Riot sometimes had to work at being outrageous with wild clothes and stuff, but in this band we can just be what we are and people will remember us because there's so much insanity going on among the four of us."

While videos have gained Quiet Riot a huge new following, the group still feels its basic appeal is in live performances. "We're an arena rock band," says Kevin. They were planning a tour which Kevin insists is going to last "forever."

To get in touch with Quiet Riot write:

Pasha/CBS
1801 Century Park West
Los Angeles, CA 90067

ADAM ANT

A lot of artists resent videos. Not Adam Ant. "Video is a new generation, as drastically new as, say, punk was to rock 'n' roll. I'm from a generation that started in 1977, and all I'm trying to do is, rather than wallow in the past, get on with the future. Video has been largely ignored as a serious art form for years. And it's still an all-out battle to do work that is legitimate—that's what I'm trying to do. It's not a promotional video— it's a film."

Adam Ant—born Stuart Goddard—had been kicking around in the music business for years without much recognition. He'd been with a number of different bands and adopted a bunch of different looks. Then, in the late seventies, his band called Adam and the Ants became leaders in what was known as the new romantic movement. Adam dressed as a pirate or an eighteenth-

Adam Ant
Allan Ballard, Epic Records, Courtesy Ant Marco Enterprises, Ltd.

century highwayman. Sometimes he called himself Prince Charming. He really looked the part. The elegant clothes, coupled with Adam's own stunning good looks, made him a natural for videos. And it was the videos that made him a big star in Britain.

When MTV started in the U.S., it began screening Adam Ant videos almost from the first day. Adam himself appeared as MTV's first guest VJ. Once the girls got a look at Adam in action, record sales soared.

Some of his videos, like "Prince Charming" and "Stand and Deliver," are still considered among the most beautiful ever made.

To contact Adam Ant write:

Epic Records
51 West 52nd Street
New York, NY 10019

THOMAS DOLBY

Thomas Dolby has his own record company, called Venice in Peril. He donates royalties to a fund to save the art treasures of that city. It's an unusual cause for a rock musician. But Dolby's an unusual guy.

His father is an archaeologist, and Dolby (his real name is Thomas Morgan Dolby Robertson) spent a lot of time traveling around Europe. He taught himself to play piano and guitar.

Dolby learned to fake it well enough to be able to play jazz piano in bars and restaurants. He had picked up an interest in electronics and began experimenting with synthesizers and new recording techniques. Dolby soon got the well-deserved reputation of being an electronic whiz and he was invited to join a number of bands. He also wrote songs.

Thomas Dolby
Richard Haughton, © Press Grange Ltd., 1983

By the fall of 1980 Dolby had decided to concentrate on his solo work. Innovative as always, he did a live show described as "a bizarre hybrid of computer-generated music, video, slide and film projections . . . perhaps closer to fringe theater or performance art than rock 'n' roll." It wasn't your usual rock concert.

It's natural that the medium of videos would attract a fellow like Dolby. When he turned to videos he picked the best director he could find—

himself. Videos like "She Blinded Me with Science" and "Hyperactive" became instant classics. They are funny, and the special effects are stunning. But the effects are not just flashy showmanship. They fit well with the song.

What's next? Dolby has been talking about making full-length films. No matter what Thomas Dolby decides to do, you can bet that it will be done on his own unique and original way.

To contact Thomas Dolby write:

Capitol Records, Inc.
1750 North Vine Street
Hollywood, CA 90028

DENNIS DEYOUNG

Chicago isn't exactly the music capital of the world. Yet native Chicagoan Dennis DeYoung still makes his home in the Windy City. He says it's because he's fanatically loyal to the White Sox. Loyalty—not all that common in the music business—has been a hallmark of Dennis's career. Along with his neighbors, twins Chuck and John Panozzo, he formed a group that was first called the Tradewinds and ultimately known as Styx. That was back in 1963, when Dennis was fourteen. Styx became one of the most popular rock bands in the U.S. The group sold over twenty million records. Dennis is its lead singer/songwriter and keyboardist.

Some critics complained that Styx didn't break any new ground musically. But the band certainly appreciated the power of blending image and

Dennis DeYoung
Courtesy The Press Office, Ltd.

music. When Styx made a tour to promote their futuristic *Kilroy Was Here* album, they prepared a short film. The film illustrated the events leading up to the music and was shown just before the group hit the stage. This innovation was greeted with wild enthusiasm. A video for "Mr. Roboto," one of the album songs, helped push the single into the top ten on the charts.

After all those years and all that success, it was something of a surprise when Dennis recorded his own solo album, *Desert Moon*. Dennis arranged, produced, wrote, sang, and oversaw every detail of the record. Rumor has it that he swept out the studio after each session as well.

Chuck Panozzo, Dennis DeYoung, James Young, John Panozzo, and Tommy Shaw of Styx.
Courtesy The Press Office, Ltd.

"All I wanted to do was illustrate my own musical tastes on record," he says, "ideas that perhaps I wouldn't have done with Styx. I honestly never thought I'd make a solo album. I've always been a team player, with the Beatles as idols."

Dennis's video for the title song of *Desert Moon* is a nostalgic look back at youth. It ends with the line, "Maybe I'll go to Chicago." Dennis DeYoung never left.

To contact Dennis DeYoung write:

A & M Records
595 Madison Avenue
New York, NY 10022

BRUCE
SPRINGSTEEN

He was the last of the great rock superstars to say no to making videos. When he finally said yes, he turned out to be a brilliant video artist. Videos capture all the dynamism and energy that make Springsteen one of America's favorite live concert performers. B.V. (Before Videos) Springsteen's records sometimes sold very well but sometimes didn't sell as well as they deserved. A.V. (After Videos) Springsteen's records began to sell like crazy, and for the first time he won a Grammy Award for the Best Male Rock Vocalist in 1984.

Springsteen is the kind of artist who doesn't need hype to be good. He doesn't need fancy costumes. He has but to come out onstage in an old pair of jeans and an old shirt and start singing to send fans into a frenzy. He's got one of the best

Bruce Springsteen
Annie Leibovitz, Ltd., Courtesy Columbia Records

"The Boss" in concert.

John Bellissimo

bands in the business, too. The E Street Band can play up a storm. Bruce Springsteen and the E Street Band put on four-hour concerts. Few rock stars could keep up a pace like that without collapsing or getting sick.

Springsteen is a real musician. He's loyal to the guys in his band and always gives them credit. He's a poetic songwriter who ignores trends and goes his own way. He's a very private person. Springsteen is also a very careful artist who works hard to get his songs just right. You can listen to a great album like *Born in the U.S.A.* over and over again without getting tired of it.

Bruce Springsteen was born in Freehold, New Jersey, in 1949. Money was scarce in Springsteen's family when he was a kid, but his childhood was far from unhappy. He went through the sort of things most working-class kids and teens go through. When he grew up he wrote about his experiences. Part of the reason he's so popular is that millions of people can identify with what he has to say. He knows what he's talking about, and they know what he's talking about. Springsteen's songs about life in high school, losing a job or working on a boring one, falling in love with someone who later leaves you, or joining the army have a ring of truth.

Springsteen began his career playing in New Jersey clubs. His first album was called *Greetings from Asbury Park, N.J.* So it's no wonder he's a hero in his home state. But you don't have to come from New Jersey to love the music of Bruce Springsteen. His songs grab you and make you think. His videos grab you and make you dance. Rock fans who know good music when they hear it will tell you Springsteen is the best.

To get in touch with Bruce Springsteen write:

CBS Records
51 West 52nd Street
New York, NY 10019

ESTABLISHED STARS

Paul McCartney doesn't need videos. Paul McCartney doesn't need anything. As the most creative of the surviving Beatles he has been on the top of the music world for decades. He's probably the most famous rock star alive. And he's certainly the richest. Every song McCartney writes and every album he records is an event.

McCartney certainly hasn't ignored videos. He's made lots of them. His 1982 video for "Ebony and Ivory," featuring McCartney and another superstar, Stevie Wonder, was an early MTV favorite. "Say, Say, Say" with Michael Jackson was even more popular. The teaming of those two giants of rock was a milestone of sorts. "Say, Say, Say" was the slickest, smoothest, and most expensively produced video to that time.

McCartney's 1984 film, *Give My Regards to Broad Street,* is much more like a series of videos than like a traditional film.

The Beatles are long gone, but the Rolling Stones are still around, though Mick Jagger is past forty and drummer Bill Wyman is nearly fifty. The Stones have changed less than any other rock group. Yet they have managed to hold on to their audience. Though they don't tour often, when they do they are the highest-paid of all concert performers.

The Stones have been featured in several memorable concert films, and they have not ignored videos. Early Stones videos have been described as "shabby we-couldn't-care-less clips." In recent years, however, they have produced some elaborate videos, all of which have that slightly sinister Rolling Stones quality. Individual members of the Stones have appeared either in their own videos or as cameos in videos by other groups. Mick himself made a very entertaining video with singer Bette Midler.

Lionel Richie is basically a songwriter, one of the best. But he's also been successful on tours, and his "Can't Slow Down" brought him a Grammy Award for Best Album of 1984. He's recently made a string of beautifully produced and successful videos. Like many established stars, he's not quite at ease with the new medium.

"I try hard not to write for video, but I've

Lionel Richie

Matthew Rolston, Courtesy Kragen and Company

found it does make me zero in a little bit more on the story. I feel a song must stand up without the visual. A video can only enhance a song. I still come from the standpoint that a song must first pass the test of 'the hum.' No music, no drums, no synthesizers, just you humming. A great song is one that you can just hum."

Still, Richie's success in videos has been so great that he has been asked if he is interested in acting projects. Not long ago he would have said, no way. "But I have to admit I'm definitely interested. . . . Time will tell."

No one could ever doubt Tina Turner's dramatic qualities. She's been a dynamite concert performer for years. She was the best thing about the 1975 rock-opera film *Tommy*. Yet Tina's career had been in the doldrums until 1984, when a series of electrifying videos helped put her back where she belongs—on top. Proof that she's back on top came in February, 1985 when she won three Grammy Awards.

There was a time back in the mid-seventies when Elton John accounted for about two percent of all record sales in the world. His position isn't quite that dominant today, but he is still one of the most popular international artists, and an Elton John concert can pack a stadium anywhere in the world, including China.

Elton has always been a wonderful and very visual stage performer with his outlandish clothes and even more outlandish spectacles. Videos seem like a perfect medium for him, and that's just what they have been. In addition to many short videos, he has made a very successful album-length video called *Visions*.

Elton is known for his devotion to the game of soccer, and he toured China with the Watford Soccer Club in 1983. But Rod Stewart goes him one better: he nearly became a professional soccer player. Actually, Rod and Elton are old chums and were in a band together in the 1960s. Like Elton, Rod is a survivor and more. He has remained on or near the top for over a dozen years.

Rod is also outspoken. During the filming of one of his videos he grumbled to a TV reporter: "These directors making these promos [videos], it's like they're filming *Ben Hur* or *Gone with the Wind,* you know. I have no idea what's going on on the set, what they're doing has nothing to do with the song . . . but then, we can't worry about that, now can we?" His director rushed to say that Rod wasn't really "put off by it—just a little mystified, that's all. Which is normal." Well,

Rod Stewart
John Bellissimo, 1984

mystified or not, Rod has made a long string of energetic, entertaining, and occasionally beautiful videos.

Like Lionel Richie, Billy Joel is mainly a songwriter. And like Richie he has become an exciting stage performer and a master of the new video medium. Billy's career has had its ups and downs. The cover of his first album features him standing inside a Long Island meat locker wearing armor and animal skins. He was part of a group called Attila. The record bombed, and for a time Billy really did have to support himself playing piano in a bar. But that's all in the past. He's been on top since 1977.

While he's ordinary-looking, and not a particularly good dancer, he still makes terrific videos. It doesn't matter whether it's a video filled with strange and disturbing images like "Pressure" or something straightforward and good-natured like "Uptown Girl." For a guy who's supposed to have zero visual appeal, Billy does pretty well.

Talking Heads is not the sort of name you put up along with Paul McCartney and the Rolling Stones. Their concerts don't pack huge stadiums; their records don't sell in the millions. But, quietly, they have built a solid following among rock critics and fans. They are now one of the most respected bands in the world. They don't make many records. They don't make many videos either. But what they do is done very well

Billy Joel
Giles Larrain, Courtesy Columbia Records

indeed. Davie Bowie himself said of one of the band's videos, "For my personal taste, this is exactly what I think videos should be." High praise from a master.

In 1984 the Talking Heads concert film *Stop Making Sense* was released. It was sponsored in part by MTV. A lot of people think it may just be the best concert film ever made. In sound and sight Talking Heads are a force to be reckoned with.

FUTURE STARS

Who will be the rock video superstars of the future? That's not a question that we can really answer. That's not a question that anyone can really answer. Prediction is always a risky business. But anyone in rock will tell you that trying to predict who's going to be on top next year, or even next month, is foolish. This is doubly true now, when videos are changing the face of popular music. Who would have predicted the success of Cyndi Lauper, Boy George, or Madonna? No one. But, foolish or not, we're going to do a little predicting, or guessing anyway.

Julian Lennon's name alone is enough to get him noticed. As the son of the late John Lennon, he most certainly has a head start in rock. But the sons and daughters of other famous performers have tried to follow in the family tradition and after an initial burst of publicity they have wilted.

Holly Johnson of Frankie Goes to Hollywood as Guest VJ on MTV.

Esther Halio

Julian Lennon, however, looks like he's going to have staying power. No, he's probably not going to be as famous as his father, John. Who could be? Yet he has his own distinctive and very appealing style. His records have already hit the top of the charts. He doesn't go in for flashy, highly produced videos. Mostly it's just Julian, his keyboard, his voice, and his songs. As we said, not flashy. Maybe even a little old-fashioned. But very nice. He could be around for a long time.

The Beatles came from the English city of Liverpool. They shook up the music world. Right now another group from Liverpool is shaking up the music world in Britain and throughout Europe. They may be destined for the top in the

U.S. as well. They are called Frankie Goes to Hollywood—or the Frankies. Actually, none of them is named Frankie, and before their first U.S. tour late in 1984 none of them had ever been to Hollywood either. They picked the name from an article in an old movie-fan magazine about Frank Sinatra.

Frankie is a dramatic band with a strong and very individualistic sound. Lead singer Holly Johnson is a very ordinary-looking fellow, but when he performs he has real charisma—and a slightly sinister quality.

The group released its first single, "Relax," in Britain in October 1983, and since that time it has set all kinds of sales records. "Relax" has outsold all the Beatles' singles. And it stayed on the charts longer than any single since Frank Sinatra's "My Way," and that was way back in 1969. Their second single, "Two Tribes," also topped the charts in Britain, as did their third, "The Power of Love."

Popularity in Britain and in Europe does not automatically mean popularity in the U.S. The band has come to the U.S. armed with videos. There are several different videos for "Relax." And the videos for "Two Tribes" and "The Power of Love" are very different, very original. The Frankies performed at the MTV New Year's Eve party, and Holly Johnson has already been a guest VJ.

UB-40

Courtesy A&M Records

Frankie Goes to Hollywood has all the credentials for rock video superstardom.

Also appearing at that MTV New Year's Eve party was another British group, called UB40. This group has a mission of sorts: to establish reggae as a popular form of music in the U.S. Reggae, which began on the island of Jamaica, has become well established in Britain, but in America it has remained pretty much an imported curiosity. UB40 would like to change that. "We're a pop band in England," says UB40 drummer James Brown, "and we're in the business of making pop music. We don't want to corner the radical student market, per se; we want the normal everyday record-buying public to buy our records, and we don't care if they're Democrats or Republicans. As far as I'm concerned, reggae is an important form of pop music, and it can be as popular as rock 'n' roll or soul music or jazz. It just needs to be given the chance."

UB40, with the help of music videos, is trying to give it that chance.

Another contender for superstardom is the beautiful Sheila E. Her full name is Sheila Escovedo. Right now Sheila is best known for appearing with Prince on his Purple Rain tour. The California-born musician had previously worked with Lionel Richie's road band. She's something of a novelty—one of the few female drummers. But her solo video has shown that Sheila is not only a drummer but also has a fine singing voice and a stunning visual presence—she looks great! She has all the qualities that should make for success in the new era of rock video.

Make It Big is the title of the second album from Andrew Ridgeley and George Michael. They're better known as Wham! And make it big is just what this good-looking pair appears to be doing. Wham!'s upbeat dance tune, "Wake Me Up Before You Go-Go," aided by one of the most cheerful videos ever made, brought the pair to the attention of U.S. fans. And talk about looking

George Michael and Andrew Ridgeley of Wham!
Brian Aris © D.P.A., Courtesy Columbia Records

great! Wham! is a good bet for superstardom in the very near future.

So those are a few of our choices, our guesses. You can make your own, and we're quite sure that you will. After all, the choice as to who will be the next rock video superstars is really up to you.

The music business is usually tough and commercial. But, early in 1985, forty-five of America's top recording artists got together to shoot a video and make a single entitled "We Are The World." Among the artists were Cyndi Lauper, Bruce Springsteen, Hall and Oates, Billy Joel,

Some of the forty-five artists who recorded "We Are The World" for African famine relief.

Henry Diltz/USA For Africa

121

and Sheila E. The song was written by Michael Jackson and Lionel Richie. Every penny from the sale of the video and record will be donated to the famine and drought victims of Africa.

A group of major British artists, organized by singer Bob Geldof, had recorded "Do They Know It's Christmas?" in 1984. That record sold millions of copies worldwide, and all the profits went to African relief.

Says Geldof, "Pop music can become incredibly important when it is used as a huge moral force for good. The central thing about what people did here, and what the people in England did, is that they're making compassion hip. If audiences will get out of this the sense that it's fashionable to care—if that's absolutely *all* they get out of this—then it's worth it, time and time again."

Donations can be sent to:

USA for Africa
1112 North Sherbourne Drive
Los Angeles, CA 90069